Poems about

you and me

A collection of poems about values

Compiled by Brian Moses

Artwork by Michaela Blunden

WAYLAND

Titles in the series

Poems about **me**

Poems about **you and me**

Editor: Sarah Doughty
Designer: Tim Mayer

First published in 1998 by
Wayland Publishers Ltd
61 Western Road, Hove
East Sussex, BN3 1JD

© Copyright 1998 Wayland Publishers Ltd

British Library Cataloguing in Publication Data
Poems about you and me
    1. Children's poetry, English
    I. Moses, Brian, 1950- II. You and me
    821.9'14'08'035

ISBN 0 7502 1128 8

Printed and bound by G.Canale & C.S.p.A. Turin

Find Wayland on the Internet at http://www.wayland.co.uk

Contents

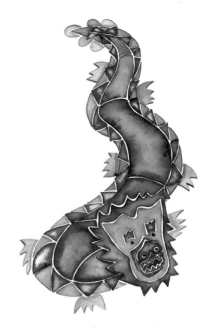

Friends

When you meet your friend,
your face brightens –
you have struck gold.

Kassia, 9th Century, Greece

With clothes the new are best;
with friends the old are best.

*traditional
China*

That's you and me!

As friends we:

whisper,
discuss,
argue
then float messages across a crowded playground
that only we know and understand.

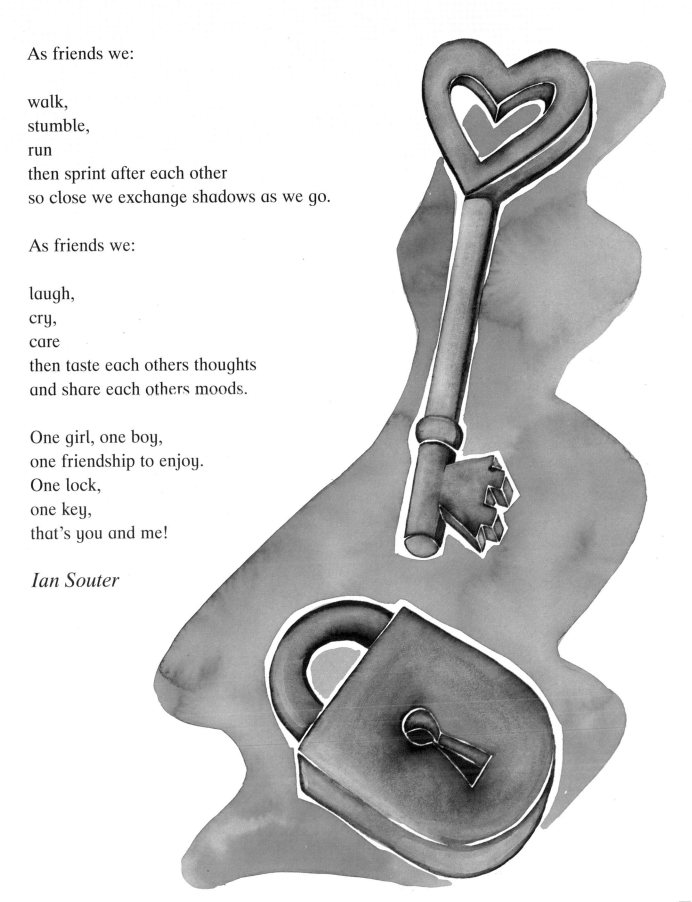

As friends we:

walk,
stumble,
run
then sprint after each other
so close we exchange shadows as we go.

As friends we:

laugh,
cry,
care
then taste each others thoughts
and share each others moods.

One girl, one boy,
one friendship to enjoy.
One lock,
one key,
that's you and me!

Ian Souter

Best friends

Would a best friend
    Eat your last sweet
    Talk about you behind your back
    Have a party and not ask you

Mine did.

Would a best friend
Borrow your bike without telling you
Deliberately forget your birthday
Avoid you whenever possible

Mine did.

Would a best friend
    Turn up on your bike
    Give you a whole packet of your favourite sweets
    Look you in the eye

Mine did.

Would a best friend say
    Sorry I talked about you behind your back
    Sorry I had a party and didn't invite you
    Sorry I deliberately forgot your birthday
    – I thought you'd fallen out with me

    Mine did.

    And would a best friend say, simply,
        Never mind
        That's O.K

I did.

Bernard Young

Two friends

Lydia and Shirley have
two pierced ears and
two bare ones
five pigtails
two pairs of sneakers
two berets
two smiles
one necklace
one bracelet
lots of stripes and
one good friendship

Nikki Giovanni

Friendship

I've discovered a way to stay friends forever –
There's really nothing to it.
I simply tell you what to do
And you do it!

Shel Silverstein

Friendship

It's playing a game
It's a chase in the park
It's a spooky story
Told after dark.

It's a birthday present
It's a helping hand,
It's always trying
To understand.

It's a tree to climb
It's a joke to share,
Friendship is someone
Who's always there.

Andrew Collett

Co-Operation

A see-saw
only works

if you've
got a friend

on the
other end.

Tony Langham

11

The new lad

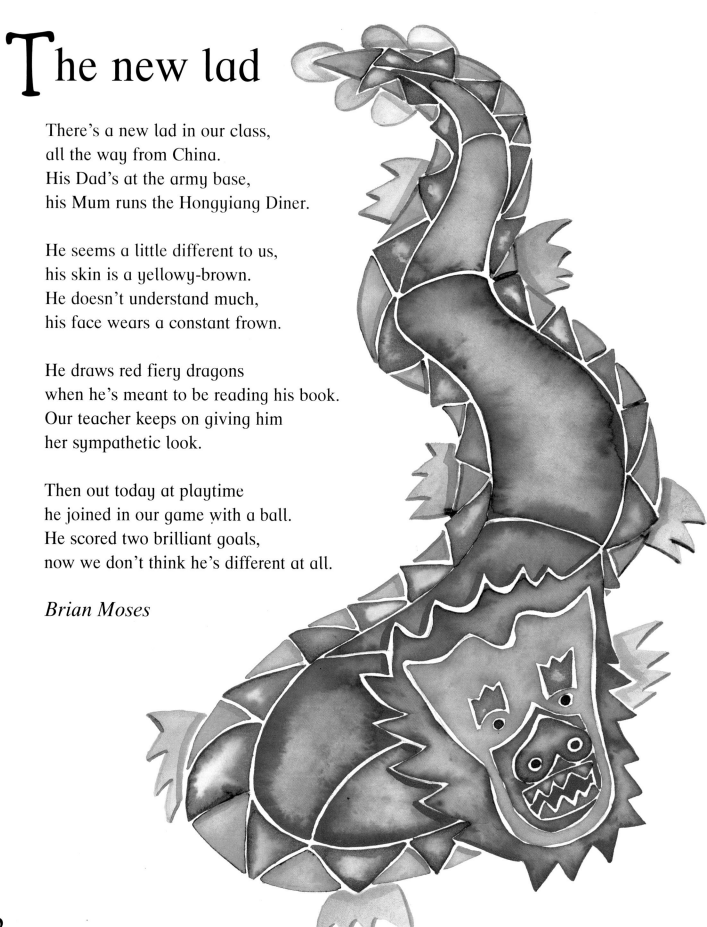

There's a new lad in our class,
all the way from China.
His Dad's at the army base,
his Mum runs the Hongyiang Diner.

He seems a little different to us,
his skin is a yellowy-brown.
He doesn't understand much,
his face wears a constant frown.

He draws red fiery dragons
when he's meant to be reading his book.
Our teacher keeps on giving him
her sympathetic look.

Then out today at playtime
he joined in our game with a ball.
He scored two brilliant goals,
now we don't think he's different at all.

Brian Moses

Faisal

My mate Faisal
can't walk by himself,
can't talk by himself,
can't hold a pencil by himself,
can't go to the toilet by himself.

He can't do lots of things.

But he's got a machine
on his wheelchair
that talks for him
when he moves his head
from side to side.

And every morning
at 9 o'clock
when we meet
in the school corridor
he makes the machine say –

"Hiya, Liam! Got any
spots on your belly?"

That makes me laugh.

That's something
Faisal can do –

better than anyone else.

Tony Langham

14

Secrets

I love secrets when they belong to me,
When all my friends crowd round
And whisper quietly.

I love secrets when they belong to friends
Who say that they can't share them,
But tell me in the end.

I love secrets when they belong to Mum,
They twinkle brightly in her eyes
And promise me some fun.

I love secrets when they belong to Dad
Because he teases me with clues
And nearly drives me mad.

But I hate secrets when they snigger and
  they lie,
When they belong to someone else
Who wants to make me cry.

Coral Rumble

Break time

In break time I wander about, or stand,
Or pick up old junk like this rubber band,
Or slip round the side of the building and hide,
Or draw with my shoe in the sand.

Big gangs rush up, shouting: "Come on!
　Play schools!"
But I don't know how. I don't know the rules.
So they shout at me: "Move! Shove off!
　Get out!"
And I run off, feeling a fool.

But I've seen someone else who stands
　alone, too.
I don't know her well, but I think her name's
　Sue.
She wanders around with her eyes on the
　ground.
We can form our own gang – just us two!

Kate Williams

Partners

Find a partner,
says sir, and sit
with him or her.
A whisper here,
a shuffle there,
a rush of feet.
One pair,
another pair,
till twenty-four
sit safely on the floor
and all are gone
but one
who stands,
like stone,
and waits;
tall,
still,

alone.

Judith Nicholls

Left out

It feels as if pins
Are pricking my eyes.
My face is burning hot.
A firework is trying
To go off inside me.
My feet are glued to the spot.
My hands are rocks in my pockets.
I want to run away,

But my legs are rooted to the ground
Like trees. I have to stay
And listen
To everyone calling me names
And not letting me
Join in with their games.

Celia Warren

Name-calling

They called me frog-face with ears like a bat.
I said, 'I'm not – I'm worse than that.'

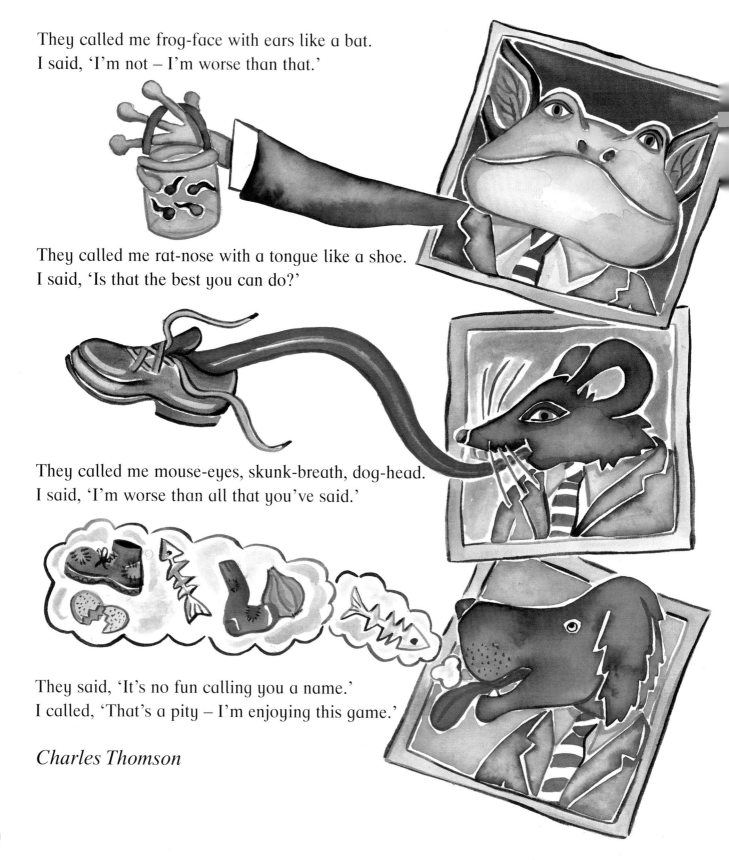

They called me rat-nose with a tongue like a shoe.
I said, 'Is that the best you can do?'

They called me mouse-eyes, skunk-breath, dog-head.
I said, 'I'm worse than all that you've said.'

They said, 'It's no fun calling you a name.'
I called, 'That's a pity – I'm enjoying this game.'

Charles Thomson

Calling names

I call my brother
Waggle Ears, Banana Boots
and Nobble Nose.

He calls me Mop Head,
Turnip Top,
Potato Pie and Twinkle Toes.

I call him Weed,
he calls me Wimp
then Mum comes in the door.

She calls us Double Trouble
then we're both
good friends once more.

Irene Rawnsley

Breaking friends with Sharon

I've broken friends with Sharon
she's broken friends with me.
I told her I don't like her,
she said she doesn't like me.
Sharon's really silly
Sharon never shares,
snatches pens and peanuts
Sharon even swears.

Sharon – we don't play now
Sharon plays with Jo
and I don't go to netball –
– not if Sharon goes.

She told Miss Andrews of me,
she told my sister lies.
I think her new coat's awful
her face,
her smile
and eyes.
I think she's really nasty,
I'd love to see her go,
but one thing's really awkward . . .
what if she says –
'Hello'

Peter Dixon

Since Hanna moved away

The tyres on my bike are flat.
The sky is grouchy gray.
At least it sure feels like that
Since Hanna moved away.

Chocolate ice cream tastes like prunes.
December's come to stay.
They've taken back the Mays and Junes
Since Hanna moved away.

Flowers smell like halibut.
Velvet feels like hay.
Every handsome dog's a mutt
Since Hanna moved away.

Nothing's fun to laugh about.
Nothing's fun to play.
They call me, but I won't come out
Since Hanna moved away.

Judith Viorst

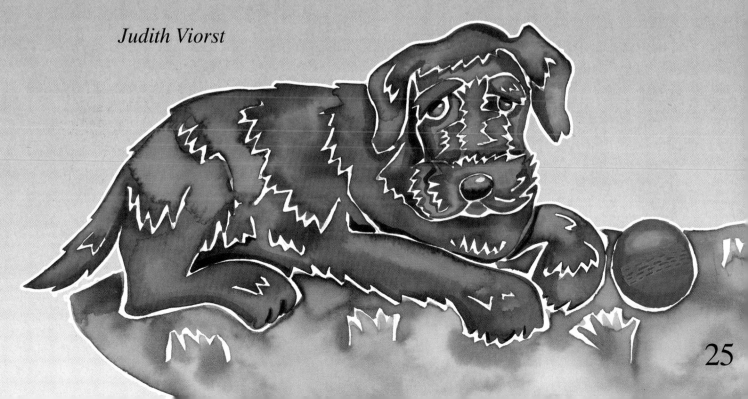

Trouble

When cheeky First Years
In the yard
start acting hard
They soon find out
I'm trouble.

Choosing
A football team at school?
Make me the Captain!
That's the rule,
Or I'll make trouble.

Those sweets you've brought
To give away;
Remember,
I'm your best friend today,
Or there'll be trouble.

Nobody refuses me a thing;
I'm always the boss,
The ace, the king.
Try me.
I'm trouble.

Irene Rawnsley

The bully

You know it's quite a mystery
why Glenford likes to bully me
when I've done nothing at all
he pushes me and then I fall.
At playtime sitting on the benches
he showers me with spiteful punches.
Teacher, Teacher can't you see?
How Glenford Lewis bullies me?
He says that if I ever tell
both my cheeks are sure to swell.
Things could not get much worse. . .
so I think I'll tell my parents first.

Pauline Stewart

Letter to a superhero

Dear Captain Meteorite,

Help! Gary Pritchard's bullying me.
He bullies lots of kids in my school,
but he picks on me most of all.
Do you think you could take time off
from fighting the mega-evil Dr. Snarg
and his incredible Slime Bandits
and come and help me instead?
I know you'll have to travel
half-way across the Universe,
but if you could come, I'd be very grateful.
Do you think you could get here
before playtime on Monday morning?

I don't want you to hurt Gary.
I'm sure you won't have to.
I just want you to tell him
to stop bullying me – or else
you'll vaporise him
with your Zapp Gun.
That should make him stop.
Thanks a lot.
Watch out for Black Holes!

Best wishes,

Benjamin

28

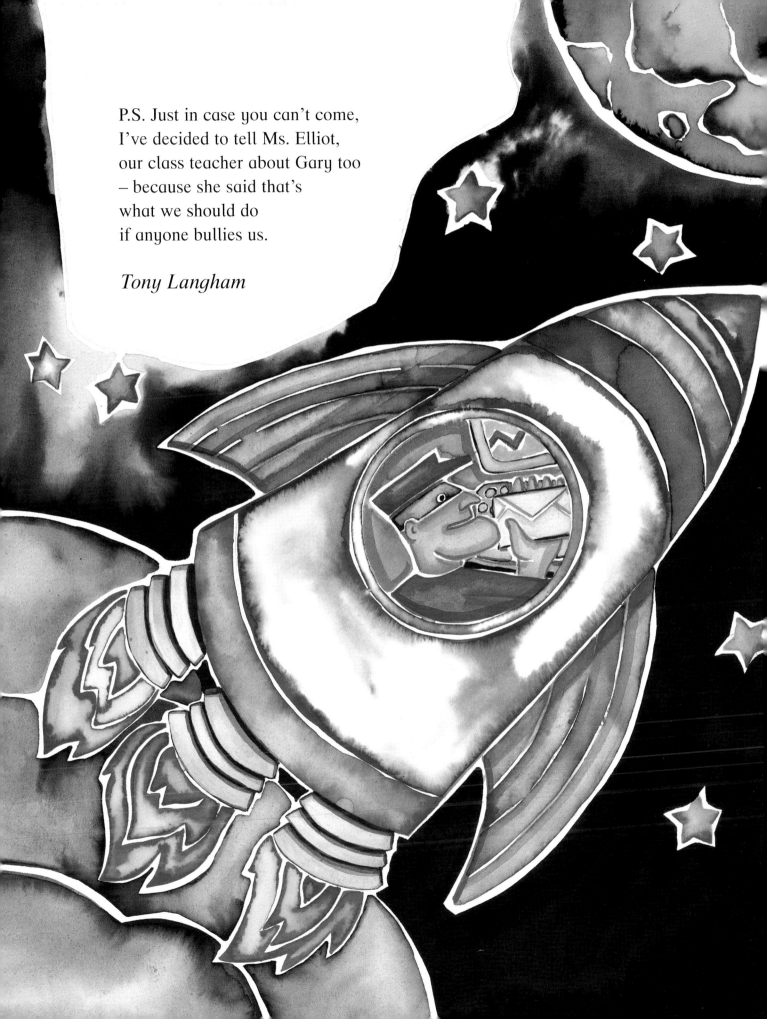

P.S. Just in case you can't come,
I've decided to tell Ms. Elliot,
our class teacher about Gary too
– because she said that's
what we should do
if anyone bullies us.

Tony Langham

Notes for parents and teachers

It is hoped that the poems in this book will help children to be aware of different relationships, and to realize that they need to modify their own behaviour in response to the needs and demands of others. There should be plenty of time for talking about the poems and discussing how far the ideas expressed relate to children's own circumstances. It is anticipated too, that many of these poems may be presented to children as stimulus or models for their own writing.

The poet Brian Jones once wrote in his poem 'About Friends' –

> The good thing about friends
> is not having to finish sentences.

What do children understand by this, and do they agree that it's true? Suggest that they examine the poems about friendship at the start of this book and find other lines that seem to sum up what friendship is all about. Can they go on to write their own definitions of friendship? What about Shel Silverstein's poem? Can this ever form the basis for real friendship?

Look at the poem 'Co-operation'. Can children think of other instances where it is difficult or impossible to do something properly without someone else being involved? Perhaps these ideas could be written into a poem.

> On my own I couldn't
> play tennis or snap.
> On my own a bike ride
> just isn't the same.
> On my own ...

Friends quite often share the same interests, but what about those children who are a little different or who don't make friends easily?

Read the poems 'The New Lad', and 'Break Time'. Suggest that children write a story or act out a play about someone who is new to their school and who finds it hard to fit in. What positive things can be done to make that person feel welcome?

Some of the poems in this collection have patterns where one or more phrases of lines are repeated to help strengthen the rhythm. In Andrew Collett's 'Friendship' it is the 'It's ...', in Bernard Young's 'Best Friends' it is the question, 'Would a best friend ...', and in Judith Viorst's 'Since Hanna Moved Away', the title is repeated as the final line in each verse. Some children may enjoy reading these poems aloud and listening out for the rhythm. Others may like to add a background of percussion instruments to a rendition of a poem.

Consider the poems about name calling and bullying. How should children react to bullying? Suggest that children write Captain Meteorite's reply to Tony Langham's 'Letter to a Superhero'. What sort of advice would he give to a victim of bullying? In Celia Warren's 'Left Out' she describes how it feels to be unwanted. Have children ever been in a similar situation? Does anyone want to write about how they felt? (Indicate that anything written down would only be read by the teacher/parent.) Such writing can act as powerful therapy for some children.

Suggest that children look through poetry books to find other poems on the subject areas that are covered in this collection. Make up class anthologies on specific themes. Talk about the poems and what children like about them.

Books to read

The following books may be useful to use alongside the poems featured in this collection:

PLEASE MRS. BUTLER and I HEARD IT IN THE PLAYGROUND both by Alan Ahlberg, (Puffin).
More poems on the nature of friendship particularly 'Small Quarrel' and 'It is a Puzzle' in the former, and 'The Boy Without a Name' in the latter.

MY BEST FIEND, TROUBLE WITH THE FIEND, THE FIEND NEXT DOOR and other books by Sheila Lavelle (Puffin).
Very funny series of books about Angela who is always having fiendish ideas and getting her friend Charlie into trouble.

BEST FRIENDS FOREVER by Kathryn Cave (Puffin, 1995).
Sam and Alex have always been best friends. Then Emma joins the class and the boys argue about who should look after her.

HOW TO WRITE REALLY BADLY by Anne Fine (Mammoth, 1996).
Explores the nature of friendship between new boy Chester and Joe, 'the Writer from Hell'.

THE WILLOW STREET KIDS: BEAT THE BULLIES by Michele Elliott (Macmillan, 1997).
In a situation where they are being bullied should the Willow Street kids 'tell' and if they do, will it make life any easier for them?

BULLIES AT SCHOOL by Theresa Breslin (Blackie, Thriller Firsts, 1993).
Siobhan is teased by her classmates and desperately unhappy until she discovers a Celtic brooch that gives her a strange new power.

Acknowledgements

The author and publishers would like to thank the poets and their agents for allowing their poems to be used in this anthology. Although every attempt has been made to contact the owners, if we have been unable to contact copyright holders we apologise for this apparent negligence.

'Friendship' from A LIGHT IN THE ATTIC by Shel Silverstein. Copyright © 1981 by Evil Eye Music, Inc. By permission of Edite Kroll Literacy Agency Inc.

Picture acknowlegements:
Bubbles 6 (Roger Livermore), 17 (James Lamb), 18/19 (Loisjoy Thurston), 12 (Ian West), 26 (Nikki Gibbs); Tony Stone Worldwide cover, 5 (Lori Adamski Peek), 8/9 (Lori Adamski Peek), 13 (David Madison), 24 (Peter Cade), Wayland Picture Library 15, 16, 21, 27.

Index of first lines